To the reader:

Welcome to the DK ELT Graded Readers! These readers are different. They explore aspects of the world around us: its history, geography, science … and a lot of other things. And they show the different ways in which people live now, and lived in the past.

These DK ELT Graded Readers give you material for reading for information, and reading for pleasure. You are using your English to do something real. The illustrations will help you understand the text, and also help bring the Reader to life. There is a glossary to help you understand the special words for this topic. Listen to the cassette or CD as well, and you can really enter the world of the Olympic Games, the *Titanic*, or the Trojan War … and a lot more. C interest you, improve your English, and all at the same time.
Enjoy the series!

GW00492581

To the teacher:

This series provides varied reading practice at five levels of language difficulty, from elementary to FCE level:
BEGINNER
ELEMENTARY A
ELEMENTARY B
INTERMEDIATE
UPPER INTERMEDIATE
The language syllabus has been designed to suit the factual nature of the series, and includes a wider vocabulary range than is usual with ELT readers: language linked with the specific theme of each book is included and glossed. The language scheme, and ideas for exploiting the material (including the recorded material) both in and out of class are contained in the Teacher's Resource Book. We hope you and your students enjoy using this series.

A DORLING KINDERSLEY BOOK

DK www.dk.com

Originally published as Eyewitness Reader
Secrets of the Mummies in 1998 and adapted
as an ELT Graded Reader for
Dorling Kindersley by

studio cactus ©

13 SOUTHGATE STREET WINCHESTER HAMPSHIRE SO23 9DZ

Published in Great Britain by
Dorling Kindersley Limited
9 Henrietta Street, London WC2E 8PS

2 4 6 8 10 9 7 5 3 1

Copyright © 2000
Dorling Kindersley Limited, London

A CIP catalogue record for this book is
available from the British Library.

ISBN 0-7513-3193-7

Colour reproduction by Colourscan, Singapore
Printed and bound in China
by L. Rex Printing Co., Ltd
Text film output by Ocean Colour, UK

The publisher would like to thank the following
for their kind permission to reproduce their photographs:
c=centre; t=top; b=below; l=left; r=right

AKG London Ltd: Erich Lessing 12tl; The Ancient Art
and Architecture Collection: Ronald Sheridan 3b, 17bl,
20t; Bridgeman Art Library, London: Egyptian National
Museum 17cla; Louvre/Giraudon 7bcr; by kind permission
of the Trustees of the British Museum: 4tl, cl, 5tr, br, 6cl,
7tr, 8–9bc, 8tl, bl, 9tr, cr, 10l, 12bl, 13cr; Bruce Coleman
Collection: Joe McDonald 18tl; Colorific!: Kirsten P.
Head 14cl; Mary Evans Picture Library: 20tl; Forhistorisk
Museum, Moesgard, Denmark: 4–5b; Robert Harding
Picture Library: 15tr, 16cl, 17b, tr; Walter Rawlings 17cl;
Michael Holford: 12b, Hulton Getty Collection: 14tl,
16tl; Pelizaeus-Museum, Hildesheim, Germany: 7c, cb;
Reunion des Musées Nationaux: Louvre 11tr; Sygma:
L'Illustration 19bl
Jacket credit:
British Museum/Dorling Kindersley/Peter Hayman

Contents

ELT Graded Readers

UPPER INTERMEDIATE

MUMMY MYSTERIES

Written by David Maule

Series Editor Susan Holden

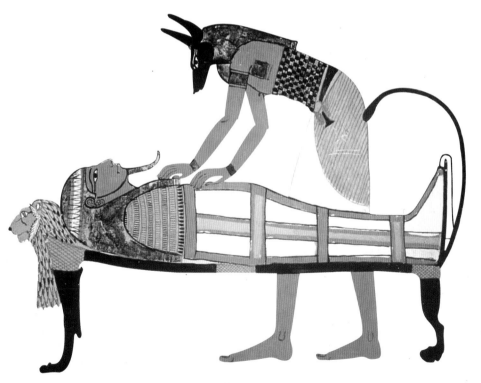

London • New York • Delhi • Sydney

Teenage boy
Some Roman mummies were decorated with a realistic painting of the person who had died.

Animals
The ancient Egyptians treated cats like gods. They often mummified cats' bodies when they died.

People from the Past

Mummies are interesting for many different reasons. We all know we are going to die, so we think about death from time to time. We may have different ideas about what we will experience after death, but we know what will happen to our bodies. Most will be burned, or buried, and allowed to decay. However, a few people over the centuries have managed to cheat this process. They have become mummies.

Sometimes this has happened naturally. Well-preserved bodies have been dug out of bogs in various countries, especially Denmark. In certain types of bog, there is no air below the surface, and hardly any decay takes place. The skin of these bodies looks rather like leather but the long-dead faces are recognizable. Scientists can discover many things about the way they lived and the way they died. Bodies have also been found in hot, dry deserts and on icy mountains.

For bodies to decay, both air and water are needed. Take away one of these, and the process can be slowed down or even stopped. This was discovered centuries ago, and various peoples mummified their dead for religious reasons.

The most famous of these were the ancient Egyptians. But other peoples, such as the Incas of South America and the Pazyryks of Siberia, also used to preserve dead bodies. These societies believed that it was important to preserve the body for a life after death, and the mummies were usually buried with things to take with them: bowls, statues, jewellery, and so on. Of course, the process of mummification takes time and a lot of work, and so costs money. It was only for the rich. Ordinary people had to take their chance after death.

In more recent times, some bodies have been preserved, not to improve their own position in the afterlife, but to influence those who are still alive. Later, we shall look at two very famous people who were mummified after they died – Lenin and Evita Perón. But first, let us look at how the ancient Egyptians made a mummy.

This mummy was found in a Danish bog. It is the body of a man who died more than 1,500 years ago.

Objects
Everyday things were often buried with mummies.

Important doll
Figures, such as this Peruvian doll, were buried with a mummy to bring the dead person luck in the afterlife.

Making a Mummy

Temple guardians
A chief priest represented the king and the gods. He looked after the temple and performed religious ceremonies.

An Egyptian priest

Embalming
This means using chemicals or perfumes to stop a body from decaying, or breaking down.

The ancient Egyptians had one of the greatest civilizations the world has ever known. Everybody has heard of the buildings they left behind. The pyramids are only the most famous of many others. The ancient Egyptians' civilization lasted for 3,000 years – a thousand years longer than the time from the birth of Christ to now.

These people had strong beliefs about gods and life after death. They believed that if a dead person's spirit could recognize its preserved body, it would live forever in the afterlife. This belief has given us another item that we connect with ancient Egypt – mummies.

This, however, was only for the rich, because only rich people could afford the process of mummification. It was done by special priests, and people also believed that, if the priests said the right prayers, this would help to decide what happened to the person's spirit after death.

As soon as the person died, a servant would go to the chief priest. The other priests would be called, and they would all go to their workshop on the west bank of the River Nile.

At the same time, other servants would go to the house of the dead person, collect the body and take it to the workshop. Everything had to be done very quickly because Egypt is a hot country and the process of decay happens fast. Today, in many hot countries, there is a rule that bodies must be buried or burned within 24 hours of death.

At the workshop, the body was laid on a special table, ready for the ceremony to begin. The chief priest would put on a special mask, shaped like the head of a jackal. This was to represent Anubis, the god of mummification. Then, he would slowly wash the body while another priest read out religious phrases from a special book. When the body was clean enough, the embalming process could begin.

First, one of the priests took a long, thin metal hook and pushed it slowly up the body's nose. He used the hook to break through the bone between the top of the nose and the brain. Then he took another hook, pushed this up the nose in the same way, and pulled out some of the brain. He did the same thing again and again, until the skull was empty.

Tools
These tools were used in a process which people thought would help the mummy to eat and drink in the afterlife.

This ancient Egyptian painting shows a body being washed.

After being washed, the body was left to dry.

Jackal mask
At embalming ceremonies, jackal-headed masks, like this clay one, represented Anubis, god of mummification.

7

All of these pieces of brain were simply thrown away because the priests did not understand what it was for. They thought the heart was the centre of thinking, and of feeling. The heart was left inside the body when the other organs were removed.

Before this, the mouth was cleaned, and filled with pieces of cloth, and the nose was filled with wax. A small piece of cloth was placed over each eye, and the eyelids were pulled shut over them.

The next job was not done by a priest, because it was seen as dirty. A man came into the workshop and used a very sharp stone to cut through the skin down one side of the body.

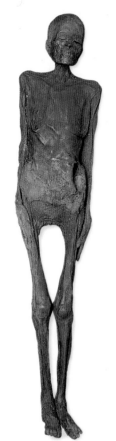

Incision
A cut was usually made down the left side of the body.

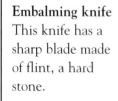

Embalming knife
This knife has a sharp blade made of flint, a hard stone.

Hapy was a baboon god who guarded the lungs.

The falcon god Qebehsenuef guarded the intestines.

Then he removed the stomach, liver, lungs, and intestines. As each of these came out it was wrapped in cloth and put in a canopic jar – a special container made in the shape of a god.

This was the end of the first part of the process. Apart from the heart, everything from inside the body had been taken out, leaving only skin, flesh, and bones. Next, the body had to be dried, because fluid speeds up decay. In much the same way as people today put down salt to suck spilled wine out of a carpet, the priests used a natural salt called natron. This was piled up over the body. It would take 40 days to dry it out completely. Only then would it be ready for the next step.

Natron
This natural salt is found by the edges of desert lakes.

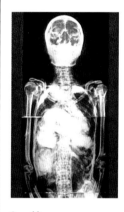

Stuffing
This X-ray of a mummy shows linen stuffing replacing some of the organs.

Sons of Horus
The four gods who guarded canopic jars were the sons of Horus, god of the sky.

Imsety was a human-like god who guarded the liver.

The jackal-headed god Duamutef guarded the stomach.

Religious figures
These figures lay on the body to guard the places where the organs had been removed.

Scarab beetle

Wadjet eye

Amulets
These were worn for good luck. People believed the wadjet eye kept bad things away.

When the body was dry, the priests removed the natron. Without fluid, it had become much thinner. They opened up the cut along the side, and filled up the space. Various materials might be used – cloth, sawdust, or even sand. Then they sewed up the cut. The process here is similar to stuffing a turkey, and done for the same reason – to help the body keep its shape. After 40 days under salt, the skin was very dry. The priests fetched oils and spices and rubbed them into the skin to keep it from cracking.

Then, the chief priest was ready to begin wrapping the body. He took thin pieces of cloth and wound them around each finger in turn. Then, more cloth was wound around the arms and legs. Finally, the whole body was wrapped up. In all, about 140 metres of cloth was used.

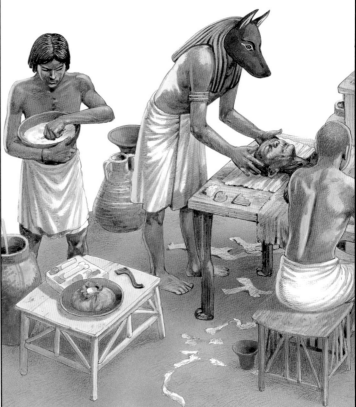

As the bandages were put on, the priests brushed them with resin – the sap of pine trees – to make them stick together. When the resin dried, it would set hard and stiff. They also stopped sometimes to say religious words or hold special ceremonies. At certain places in the bandages, small pieces of jewellery with a religious meaning were placed. Some of the bandages also had religious writing on them. The whole process was very complex, and it took seventy days from the time of the death until the wrapping was finished. You can see now why mummification was only for the rich – it kept a whole team of priests busy for over two months. It cost a great deal of money.

At the end of all of this, the bandaged body was placed in a coffin.

Nest of coffins
Sometimes, the coffin was put into a bigger coffin, which might then be put into an even bigger coffin, and so on.

Scribes
In ancient Egypt, only scribes could write. They were highly respected people.

A scribe, or writer, then handed the priest a book. Ancient Egyptian books were made of papyrus, a type of paper made from reeds. This was stuck together into a long roll. This book was called The Book of the Dead. This was placed inside the coffin.

The ancient Egyptians believed that dead people had to read the book to be safe on their journey to the Hall of the Two Truths.

This was where the destination of the dead person was decided. The god Osiris watched over everything. In the hall was a large set of scales. The dead person's heart was placed on one side and "the feather of truth" on the other.

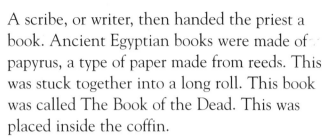

Hapy, the baboon god

Figures of fear
Figures like this hippo were put in the tomb to frighten people away.

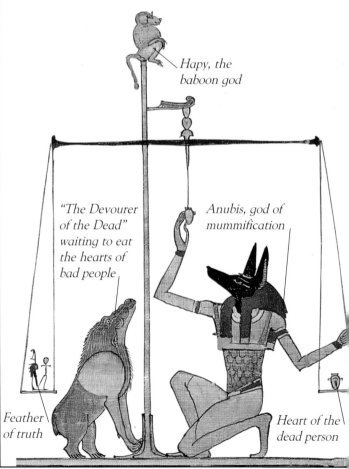

"The Devourer of the Dead" waiting to eat the hearts of bad people

Anubis, god of mummification

Feather of truth

Heart of the dead person

Anubis, the jackal-headed god of mummification, watched the scales carefully. The dead person had to answer questions about the bad things they had done. This was to see how heavy their heart was. If it was not too full of bad things, the person was allowed to live in the afterlife.

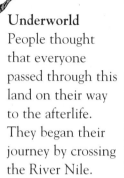

Back in this world, the dead person's family filled a tomb with food and treasures for the mummy to use in the afterlife. They believed that you could use things you owned on earth after death. For this reason, Egyptian tombs usually contained valuable objects. This made them a great target for grave robbers.

The families tried to prevent this happening in a number of ways. Tombs were built in a way that made them very difficult to get into. Often, there were hidden passages that led to the room where the coffin lay. Things were written on the walls, telling robbers of the terrible bad luck that would come their way if they stole anything. Horrible carved figures were put in different places to frighten them.

None of these things worked, of course. Over the centuries, robbers broke into many tombs looking for valuable things. They even broke into the pyramids where the pharaohs were buried. Because pyramids were so obvious, later pharaohs turned to much less public tombs cut into natural rock, usually entered by a small hole. But all of these were found and robbed – except one.

Nobody knew for certain, but many people believed that somewhere in the Valley of the Kings lay an untouched tomb, filled with unbelievably valuable objects. This was the tomb of the young king Tutankhamun.

Underworld
People thought that everyone passed through this land on their way to the afterlife. They began their journey by crossing the River Nile.

God of death
Osiris was king of the afterworld. People thought the afterworld was like Egypt, but better.

13

The Mummy's Curse

Howard Carter
Carter travelled to Egypt as a young artist and became interested in investigating ancient Egypt.

Pharaoh
The pharaohs were the kings of ancient Egypt. The people believed them to be living gods.

Howard Carter was a man with one idea in his mind. He wanted to find the tomb of Tutankhamun. This pharaoh had died young, and his tomb had been so well hidden that no grave robber had ever found it. There were stories of great treasures hidden there, and Carter was warned of the curse: "Death comes on wings to he who enters the tomb of a pharaoh."

He was looking in Egypt's Valley of the Kings. In the rocks and cliffs there are many openings, the entrances to tombs of pharaohs and other rich people, all robbed many centuries ago. Carter's men dug in the heat and the dust for five years, but found nothing.

All the work they did was paid for by a wealthy Englishman, Lord Carnarvon. But even he felt now that nothing would be found. He called Carter to his castle in England, and told him that there could be no more money.

However, while still in England, Carter was looking over some maps one night, and noticed a small area that had not been dug. It was near the entrance to a large tomb, of Ramesis VI, and seemed unlikely. But he persuaded Lord Carnarvon to pay for one last season of digging, and returned to Egypt.

On November 1, 1922, Carter and his men started clearing the area. Three days later, as they dug away some small stones, a spade hit something solid. It was a stone step cut into the rock. They kept digging and uncovered 15 more. At the bottom there was a door with royal markings on it. Could it be the entrance to Tutankhamun's tomb?

Tutankhamun
This pharaoh ruled from around 1336 BC to 1327 BC. He was probably around 16 years old when he died.

Valley of the Kings
To avoid grave robbers, many pharaohs chose this remote place for their tombs.

Carnarvon
This rich English lord visited Egypt for his health. He became interested in tombs as a way to pass the time.

Hieroglyphs
Each symbol in this ancient Egyptian writing stands for a word or a sound.

Carter said later that he found it difficult not to break the door down, there and then. But he felt that this would not be fair to Lord Carnarvon. He went to Luxor, the nearest city, and sent a telegram telling him the good news. Back at the tomb, the workmen filled up the stairs with stones again. Carter put guards there to keep thieves away, and waited.

Today, you could catch a plane from England and be in Egypt within six hours. In 1922, it was different. Although there were aeroplanes, most people still had to travel by ship. It was three weeks before Carnarvon reached Luxor.

The next day, the workmen dug out the stones again, and the two men went down the steps. Both were excited. But when they looked at the door more closely, they realized something that Carter hadn't noticed before – the door had been forced open, and closed again. Somebody had been there before them, perhaps thousands of years before.

They came to another door. To their disappointment, they saw that this one, too, had been forced open and closed again. Carter, whose hands were shaking, made a small opening in the door. He held a candle to this and looked inside. At first it was difficult to see, but as his eyes got used to the light, he began to see – in his own words – "strange animals, statues, and gold – everywhere the glint of gold."

He was so excited that, for a while, he couldn't speak. In the end, Carnarvon asked, "Can you see anything?"

"Yes," answered Carter. "Wonderful things."

He gave Lord Carnarvon the candle.

This door was broken down as well, and the men entered the room. It was packed with valuable things, but everything looked quite untidy. Thieves had been there, but it seemed they had been chased away and very little had been taken. The pharaoh's chair was there, made of gold and silver. There was a golden cabinet holding his canopic jars, each one made of gold. There were model boats, one of them set with many valuable stones, small statues of his servants, boxes containing his clothes and hundreds of other things.

The two men were astonished. When they got to the far side of the room, they found another closed door. They wanted to know what was on the other side of this. But first, everything would have to be carefully packed and sent to Cairo.

The paintings on this treasure chest show Tutankhamun defeating his enemies.

Tomb jewels
This vulture represented the goddess Nekhabet, and this scarab beetle represented the sun god Khepri.

Afterlife of luxury
The ancient Egyptians filled the king's tomb with treasure, such as golden sandals and precious jewels, for him to use in the afterlife.

When Carter returned to his house that night, he found his servants were very excited and afraid. There was a lot of shouting going on.

"What's wrong?" he said.

"You have opened the tomb," one of them said, "and brought bad luck to us."

He told Carter that a cobra had swallowed his pet canary. Carter had bought the bird because he hoped that its song would cheer up his empty house. It had seemed like a good idea, because when he saw it, one of his servants had said, "It's a bird of gold that will bring luck. This year we will find, inshallah (God willing), a tomb full of gold." Less than a week after this, the workers discovered the entrance to the tomb. Because they didn't know whose tomb it was, they called it "the tomb of the golden bird".

On that November day, when Carter opened the tomb, a cobra came into the house and swallowed the canary. That was why the servants were shouting.

An official report from the time makes some interesting points. It says that cobras are rare in Egypt, and are seldom seen in the winter – which was when the tomb was opened. It also notes that, in ancient times, they were the symbol of royalty, and that each pharaoh wore a model of a cobra on his forehead. This was to represent his power to strike at his enemies.

However, Carter was not at all worried. The next day, he went back to the tomb and started to clear the first room.

More than a kilometre of cotton padding was used to wrap up the precious things inside.

It took three months to empty the room. By this time, news of the discovery had gone round the world. On the day they opened the third door, the room was full of invited guests. Everybody was very excited. Carter made a small opening at the top of the door and, using a torch, looked in. He was astonished. On the other side, less than a metre away, he could see a wall of solid gold. When the door was removed, Carter and Carnarvon realized that the "wall" was the front of a shrine which had been built around the coffin. It was made of wood and covered with gold, and filled most of the room.

Cairo
Egypt's capital city grew up 1,000 years after the death of the last pharaoh.

Howard Carter (left) and his assistants carefully wrap a life-size statue.

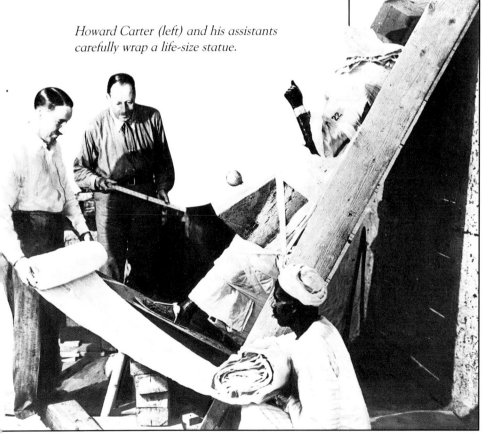

Gold cabinet
This royal shrine filled nearly all of the third room.

Kingly coffin
The middle coffin was made of wood covered with gold and pieces of glass.

The shrine had wide doors at the front. Carter removed these, and they found that inside was another shrine. When this was opened, they found a third one inside, and inside that, a fourth. This last one contained a beautiful red sarcophagus – a stone coffin. Inside this were three coffins, each shaped like a mummy. The last one held the body of King Tutankhamun.

Carter later said that opening the coffins was the most difficult job he ever did. There was very little space in front of the shrine, and the coffins fitted very tightly inside each other. Also, special oils had been poured over each one as it was placed inside, and these had now hardened and had stuck them all together.

The coffins became more and more valuable as they got smaller. The first and second one were of wood covered with gold and valuable stones. The last one was made of over 1,110 kilograms of solid gold.

It was then that, many people think, the curse of Tutankhamun struck again. Less than five months after the tomb was opened, Lord Carnarvon was bitten on the cheek by a mosquito. It raised a small lump on his cheek, and he thought nothing of it. However, the next day he cut open the bite while shaving. This became infected and Carnarvon developed a fever. Today, this could be treated, but there were no drugs that could help at the time. Lord Carnarvon became very ill. His family travelled from England to be with him. Then, early one morning, it was all over. Lord Carnarvon died.

At the very moment of his death, all the lights in Cairo went out. They stayed out for several hours, and nobody could explain why. Back at Lord Carnarvon's home in England, his dog Susie raised her ears and howled once, then died.

Other deaths followed. A French scientist who visited the tomb died after a fall. An X-ray specialist on his way to examine Tutankhamun's mummy died unexpectedly. Then, a wealthy American became ill and died after visiting the tomb. In 1972, fifty years after the tomb was opened, the British Museum asked to borrow some of the treasures for an exhibition. Many Egyptians did not think they should leave Egypt, but permission was given. One week after the Cairo museum official signed the papers which allowed the treasures to be moved, he dropped dead.

On the other hand, Carter, the man who found the tomb, lived for another eighteen years. And the man who unwrapped the mummy, Dr Douglas Derry, lived until he was well into his eighties. So, is there a curse of Tutankhamun?

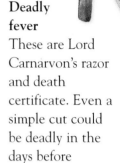

Deadly fever
These are Lord Carnarvon's razor and death certificate. Even a simple cut could be deadly in the days before modern medicines.

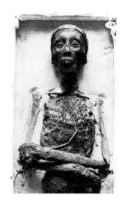

Royal mummy
Although the riches in the tomb were in good condition, Tutankhamun's mummy was badly decayed.

Inca empire
This empire covered parts of what are now Colombia, Ecuador, Peru, Bolivia, Chile, and Argentina.

Sun temples
Temples to the Sun god were built all over the empire.

Inca Emperors

As the first light of the morning sun came to the city of Cuzco, the drums started. People woke up, and they smiled and were happy. This was the 21st of June, the shortest day of the year and the most important day in the Inca empire. 500 years ago the Incas ruled a large part of South America from Colombia in the north all the way down the Andes Mountains to the southern part of Chile.

The Incas believed in the sun as the one god and they called it Inti. They believed that the sun was the father of the first Inca, Manco Capac and of his wife, Mama Ocllo Huaco. These, and their children, were sent to earth to help other people. This festival was Inti Raimi. The Incas believed that, by showing thanks and giving presents to Inti, summer would come again and their crops would grow.

Everyone in the Inca empire gave one third of all they produced to the priests of the sun god. Many of these plants and animals were given at special ceremonies held at different times of the year. The Inti Raimi ceremonies were the most important of them all.

Temples were built of carefully shaped blocks of stone. Sun temples were often filled with solid gold models of vegetables, pieces of earth, and other things connected with farming.

The ordinary people did not understand the changing of the seasons, but the priests did. They had produced a calendar which divided the year into 365 days, 12 months, and 52 weeks. The weeks were each divided into seven days of 24 hours. Each hour was made up of 60 minutes. The Inca calendar, in other words, was exactly like our own. The priests knew when the sun would begin to return, and how long each day would be.

Inca year
The Incas had a religious festival for each month. Inti Raimi was held in June, as this is the coldest month of the year in South America.

Sun disc
The Sun god was represented in many Inca temples by gold discs with human faces.

However, the giving of gifts to the sun god still continued. The priests began to say words in time to the beating of the drums. In the Holy Square, a large crowd gathered. The people were excited, but quiet and respectful. Here and there a child might cry out, but would be quietened by its parents. They were waiting for the Procession of the Living Dead.

Llamas
The llama is related to the camel. Llamas are still used in South America for wool, meat, and transport.

At last, the crowd saw the white llamas that always led the procession. There were hundreds of llamas walking in lines, one after another. Each one was beautifully brushed. Round their necks were chains of flowers, and each llama had a decorated cloth over its back. They looked proud and dignified. Perhaps they knew it was an important day.

Behi.   ie llamas came the emperor, the Sapa Inca. He sat on a litter, or platform, carried by ﹐.iests. As he came close, the people in the streets fell to their knees, hid their faces in their hands, and prayed. Ordinary people were not allowed to look at the Sapa Inca.

After him came other litters, also carried by priests. On each one was the mummified body of a former Sapa Inca. When an emperor or empress died, their internal organs were removed. Then, their body was dried using special herbs. After this, they were placed on a golden chair. With their arms crossed in front of them, and their heads looking down, they didn't look so different from when they were alive. Favourite servants would allow themselves to be killed in order to be with them in the afterlife.

Later, the mummy was carried to join its ancestors in the Temple of the Sun. On state occasions, and on religious festivals, they were taken out and carried through the streets.

The people thought of each of these as a son of the Sun god. They believed that the living Sapa Inca got help and advice from these mummies. As the mummies passed by, the people wept and called out words showing how much they respected and loved them.

Sometimes, a child might forget what its parents had said, and look up. He or she would see that each mummy wore a mask and was covered in a beautiful cloth made from the soft wool of the vicuna, a relative of the llama. But the child would not see the dead emperors' faces. These were covered in golden masks, which would protect them in the afterlife.

Litters
These beds, or stretchers, were used to carry the mummies in processions.

Huari mummy
The Huari people lived near Cuzco before the Incas. They, too, mummified their leaders.

25

Gods
Incas had great
respect for their
gods. They offered
them presents
such as statues,
gold, animals, and
sometimes even
people.

Chica
This alcoholic
drink was made
from corn. It
was stored in
decorated
clay jars.

The procession went through the city and back to the Temple of the Sun. There, the emperor moved from his litter to a golden chair and was carried into the most holy place, the Golden Courtyard. This was filled with statues of llamas and of stalks of maize, all of them made out of solid gold. White llamas were then brought in and killed, as presents to the sun.

After this, the priests blew kisses to the sun. Then there was a strange ceremony where they tried to capture the sun by tying him to a stone pillar. This was called the Intihuatana, which means "the hitching post of the sun". A hitching post is what you tie a horse to. You might remember that this festival was held in the middle of winter. Its meaning was to do with the sun not going any further away, but coming back. The people wanted the sun to return.

In the evening, the people got the chance to enjoy themselves. Midwinter festivals are common all over the world, and always have been. The early Christians decided on December as the time for the birth of Christ, because there were already festivals at that time in Europe. Different gods were involved, but the idea of the sun returning was general.

At the end of the day, the mummies were returned to their golden chairs in the Temple of the Sun. There, they had servants to look after them. In death, as in life, they sat surrounded by those who were there to help them.

The servants waved fans in the air to keep the flies off the mummies. They offered them food and water when they felt these were needed. They also delivered messages to the mummies. Somehow, they were also able to understand their replies – or, at least, people believed that they could.

For the Incas, the difference between life and death was less than it is in most societies today. It did not matter that these emperors were dead. They were still considered very powerful.

Mummified bodies
For more than 4,000 years, people across South America mummified their dead.

After the Spanish defeated the Incas in 1532, they built a church where the Temple of the Sun in Cuzco used to stand.

The Andes
This is the longest chain of mountains in the world. The Andes' snowy tops run through Peru and Chile.

Look-alike
The goddess statue was made of gold and dressed in similar clothes to the girl.

Inca Ice Girl

High in the Peruvian Andes, the snowy tops of the mountains stretched away as far as the eye could see. Down below, dark against the snow, were the moving figures of four priests, a young girl, and a number of llamas. They struggled up through the snow to the top of a high ridge, where the ground fell away on both sides.

The climbers stopped, breathing heavily, leaning on their sticks. It had taken them three days to reach the top of this mountain, Nevado Ampato. All the way, the paths had been narrow and steep, until they stopped completely. And, as they climbed higher, the air became thinner, making it more and more difficult to breathe.

The chief priest said a few words. One of the priests built a fire and started to cook a simple meal while the others unloaded the packs. They took out pots, food, small carved figures, and a statue of a goddess. Tied to the packs were some tools for digging. These were laid on the ground.

All this time the girl stood in silence, sometimes looking far down the mountain, sometimes up to its top. She was thirteen years old, and the daughter of an important Inca family. Under a warm blanket, she wore a beautiful dress of yellow, purple, and red wool, tied with a belt round her waist. The priests came and stood around her. One of them knelt in front of her, with food and drink on a tray. The girl took off the blanket she was wearing and another of the priests placed a decorated cloth over her shoulders. He fastened this with a silver pin.

Then, while he said special prayers, the chief priest placed a large headdress made of feathers on her head. The feathers were gold in colour, and her head looked like the sun was shining all around it. She looked magnificent.

Headdress
The feathers came from the macaw, a type of parrot. These feathers were often used in religious ceremonies.

Last resort
The Incas stored food in case it didn't rain. When the food ran out, they tried to make the gods happy again.

Llama food
Statues were often used in ceremonies. This llama statue may have reminded the gods to provide grass for their llamas to eat.

The chief priest said something to the girl. She smiled and sat down to eat the food. The chief priest then looked around until he found what he wanted – a hollow in the ground which was clear of snow. He pointed to it and they all started to dig using the tools they had brought with them.

They had come to the mountain because down below, in the valley where they lived, there had been very little rain for the past three years. The crops had died in the fields because they had no water and the people were starving. The priests believed that the gods were angry and had stopped the rain falling.

They had talked about it, and prayed, and talked again. Finally, they had decided that a special present had to be given to the mountain god. The present had to be the most valuable thing, a human being, and as perfect as possible. This was because whoever was chosen would live forever with the gods in the afterlife. They felt that this would please the gods and bring rain.

The girl and her family were a little frightened when she was chosen. However, this was a great honour, and they would never have thought of refusing.

Now the girl had finished her food, and went and sat near the fire. She drew her knees up to her chest and folded her arms. It was almost as if she was already dead.

The priests dug down until they had made a hole over a metre deep, and just as broad. They had brought sacks of red earth with them, which was considered very holy. They stuck this against the sides of the hole. Inside the hole they placed cups, pots and food for the girl to use in the afterlife.

Now everything was ready. The chief priest went across to the girl and held out his hand. She took it and stood up. He led her across the hole that was soon to be her grave. She sat down in front of it in the same position, with her knees drawn up. He handed her a bowl of chica, with some other drugs mixed into it. She drank it, and he gave her another.

As she drank, she gradually became unconscious. Then, she stopped breathing. The priests wrapped her body in thick cloth and lowered it into the hole. She was still in a sitting position. They filled in the hole, and continued until the girl was completely covered.

She stayed where she was for 500 years, her body frozen solid. Then, in September 1995, a volcano exploded. Hot ash fell on Nevado Ampato and melted the ice. Some scientists went to see what damage it had done, and discovered the girl's body. It had been mummified by the freezing cold. Her face had decayed but the rest of the body was still in almost perfect condition.

Mountain rescue
The two men who discovered the girl's body carried it down the mountain as fast as they could so that it would not become warm and decay. It is now kept in a freezer at a university in Peru, where it is studied and preserved.

ITALY

Palermo
SICILY

Palermo
This is the largest city on the Italian island of Sicily.

Picnics
Families often went out to visit the cemetery together, and might take a picnic lunch.

Sicilian Mummies

We are in the Sicilian city of Palermo. The year is 1926 and it is a fine, warm Saturday in spring. A family is out for a walk. The four children, two boys and two girls, are dressed in their best clothes as are the parents. This is as it should be, because the family are going to visit their relatives.

They come to the abbey of the Capuchin monks and go down a flight of stairs. At the foot, they move along a dark corridor. On either side are coffins. Some of them are opened as people look inside. Soon, the father stops. He points to a coffin. "My grandmother," he says.

The oldest girl opens the lid, as she has done before. Her great-grandmother is lying there and nothing has changed. She still looks well preserved, as she should be, because she has been mummified. Her body is one of 8,000 in the cool dark corridors below the church.

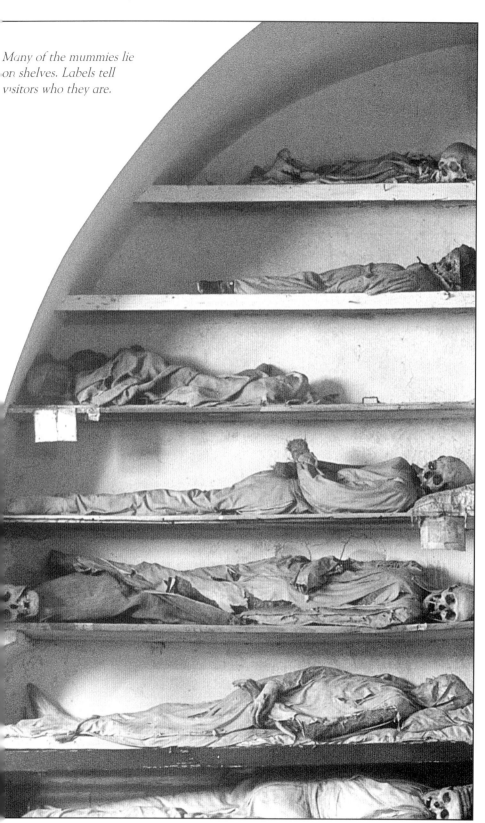

Many of the mummies lie on shelves. Labels tell visitors who they are.

33

Tourist attraction
Today, the mummies of Sicily attract thousands of visitors from all over the world.

Monk
Palermo's first mummies were the bodies of highly respected monks.

There are many coffins in the corridor, and many living people standing by them. Most of them are open at the front and stacked up, one on top of another. In each one lies a mummified body. Some are well preserved, with skin and hair still in good condition. Others are little more than dressed skeletons. The children seem to be simply curious as they look at this or that body. They do not appear to be frightened. Sometimes a child giggles, and is quietened by a word from a parent. Perhaps the child feels nervous.

The adults behave more seriously. Some are praying quietly. Others might actually be talking to a body, perhaps telling them the latest news or asking for advice. Although people are fairly quiet, everything seems normal enough. This is as it should be, because this custom has gone on for over 300 years.

Occasionally, the visitors might see a hooded figure moving silently among the coffins.

Again, they are unafraid. They know it is just one of the monks who look after the mummies.

These were Capuchin monks, who wore beards and brown robes. The church they looked after is known as an abbey. Since 1599, they had mummified the bodies of the most respected monks. These were kept in the passages cut from the rock underneath the abbey. However, it was not a secret.

Soon, local people discovered what was happening. They began asking for their relatives' bodies to be mummified as well, in return for paying some money to the abbey. They dressed the dead person in his or her best clothes before taking the body to the monks.

This practice continued up to 1881, and the custom of visiting mummified relatives grew up around it. After that time, it gradually stopped. Now, most of the people who come to see the mummies are tourists.

Monks
The monks who look after the catacomb today still wear the brown robes they have worn for hundreds of years.

Clothing
The mummies give us information about the styles of clothes people wore in the past.

Father Silvestro da Gubbio
This monk died in 1599. Every year, the monks give him a gentle dusting with a vacuum cleaner.

The monks needed over a year to mummify a body – but how it was done was kept secret for centuries!

The mummy of Father Silvestro da Gubbio is the oldest of all. When he died, his body was taken to a special cellar. There it was placed over a set of clay pipes, rather like a ladder. With dry air passing all around it, and a cool even temperature, the body began to dry out naturally. The process continued for a whole year.

Then the body was taken outside and laid in the hot Sicilian sun. By this time, the amount of water in it was much less, so that it would not begin to decay in the heat. Instead, the sun helped it to dry out completely. Then, the monks washed the body with vinegar and, last of all, wrapped it in straw and sweet-smelling herbs.

However, the process was only partly successful. Father da Gubbio's body today looks more like a dressed skeleton.

These pipes were used to drain the bodies.

And, like many of the mummies, he is not particularly attractive to look at. He stands in his space in the wall surrounded by four skulls.

As time went by, the monks improved their process of mummification. Their new methods included soaking the body in arsenic or milk of magnesia. This left the skin far softer and gave it a more lifelike colour.

Most of the bodies are not in coffins but, like Father da Gubbio's, standing up in spaces along the walls. The different passages are for different types of people. The men are divided by their jobs – monks, soldiers, lawyers, and so on. The women, who were not allowed to have jobs at that time, are separated into married or unmarried. Before they died, people might come and choose their space.

Although the monks stopped mummifying bodies in 1881, there was one later addition to the collection. Rosalia Lombardo, who died in 1920 at the age of 2, was mummified by a series of injections. Today, she looks much the same as the day she died, and is known as "The Sleeping Beauty". The doctor who invented the process also died before he could pass on the secret.

Soft skin
The mummies made in the 1800s still have their skin and hair today.

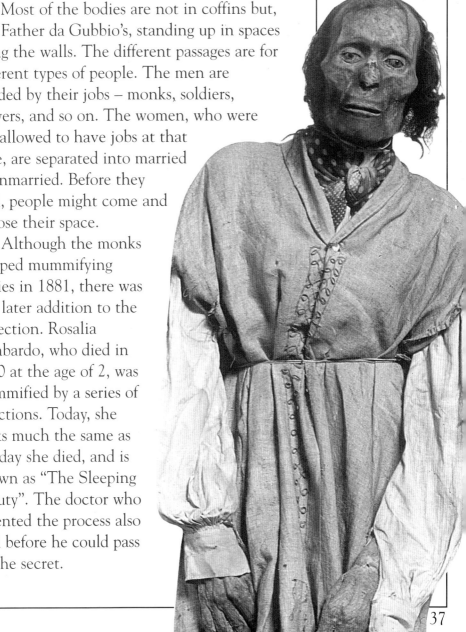

Juan Perón
Perón was the president of Argentina, the richest country in South America. Evita was his second wife.

Buenos Aires
Evita was 15 when she went to live alone in Argentina's capital city.

The Mummy Mystery

On 28 July, 1952, Dr Pedro Ara received a phone call. "Come quickly," the voice said. "Evita is dying. President Perón is asking for you."

Thunder crashed as Dr Ara hurried through the streets of Argentina's capital, Buenos Aires. After a year's illness, Evita, the president's beautiful young wife was dying. She had cancer.

From the moment her husband became president, Evita tried to help the ordinary people of Argentina. She planned and opened clinics and hospitals, and gave out food and clothes to the poor. She took action to improve housing. She got involved with trade unions who were working to get better wages for their members. Often, what she set up was badly organized, but many people got the help they needed.

She saw herself as a bridge between Juan Perón and the people of the country. She worked very long hours. Even during her last illness, when she was told to work less hard, she would answer, "I don't have time. I have too much to do."

She also helped to organize women's groups, and put pressure on the politicians so that, in 1947, Argentinian women got the right to vote. Four years later, Evita voted for the first and last time. She was so ill that she had to do this from her bed. Long before she died, she had won the hearts of many of the people of her country.

Juan Perón wanted to make sure that people never forgot his wife. Dr Ara was an expert in preserving bodies, and the president had asked him to take care of Evita's body after she died.

At 8.25 p.m., Evita died.

For the moment, the only person to know, apart from her family and the medical staff, was Dr Ara. A nurse led him down the long corridors to a room where Evita lay.

He set to work immediately. Decay begins at the moment of death, and there was no time to lose. As he began, he was aware that this was the most important job he would ever be asked to do. The results had to be first-class. Evita needed to look as if she were sleeping peacefully, but her body had to last for hundreds of years.

Dr Ara connected the tubes that were to drain all of the blood out of her body. This was replaced by glycerol, a thick liquid that would not decay. Dr Ara then placed chemicals inside the coffin to kill any insects or bacteria that might attack the body.

Dr Ara noted how much Evita had changed from the time when she was active in public life. Her face was thin, showing how much weight she had lost during her illness. It was his job to bring back as much of her beauty as possible. He worked all through the night. By dawn, the first stage was completed.

Evita was a passionate speaker, loved by many Argentinians.

Sleeping beauty
Crowds of people came to see Evita's body. Many dressed in black or wore their best clothes as a sign of respect.

Evita's body was dressed in a white gown and put into her coffin. This was fitted with a glass lid and closed tightly so that no air could get in. Then it was taken away to a place where the public could say goodbye.

Over the next sixteen days more than 2 million people chose to do so. Many were in tears. Some bent to kiss the glass lid. Dr Ara began to worry. The lid had to be lifted twice to wipe away mist on the inside. Each time, air was getting to the body, and this was not good. He knew that he had to start the next stage of the embalming process.

However, there were many who knew that Juan Perón's popularity was not as high as it once had been. He had only become President for a second time after changing the laws of the country which said that a president could only serve once, and this worried a number of people. Also, the economy was not working well at the time. The memory of Evita was useful to the Peronist party, and many of the leaders wanted to keep the body on view for as long as possible.

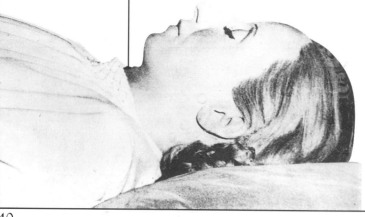

Evita looked very sick when she died. She weighed only 32 kg. But the embalming process made her look healthy again.

Dr Ara had a hard fight persuading them that he had to start work immediately, but in the end, he got his way. The body was taken to his laboratory. There, it was soaked a number of times in a bath of chemicals. It was also injected with liquids that would preserve it. Finally, it was painted with a liquid plastic. When this dried, it kept all the air out.

It took Dr Ara a year to complete the work. In the end, he was pleased with the result. He knew that the body would now stay in good condition for a long time. However, at the same time, the political situation was changing. There was growing dissatisfaction with Perón's government. In June 1955, there was a rebellion by navy and air-force officers in Buenos Aires, but the army remained loyal and the uprising didn't succeed.

There was still a lot of tension, and over the next few weeks, different groups within the government and the army, navy, and air force tried to get themselves into the best position. Finally, in September of that year, some officers started another rebellion.

The fighting lasted for three days and around 4,000 people were killed. In the end, Juan Perón had to leave. His first place of safety was a Paraguayan gunboat in Buenos Aires Harbour. After that, he left the country, first for Paraguay and later for Spain.

Nation in tears
People had to wait for hours to see Evita's body. The queue was 5 kilometres long.

Flower power
Many people bought flowers to lay near Evita's coffin. The day after she died, all the flower shops in Buenos Aires were sold out.

President Aramburu
This army general became president of Argentina after Perón left the country.

On September 20, the leader of the rebels, Major-General Eduardo Lonardi, became president. However, less than two months later, he was pushed out by another Major-General, Pedro Aramburu. This new president was very opposed to Juan Perón, and did not want anything around to remind the people of him.

He put a stop to the plans to build the Monument to the People because he didn't want Evita's body to be seen by the public. But by this time, some people had doubts about whether the body was really hers.

"It looks like a wax model," said an army officer, inspecting the mummy. He checked the fingerprints. Then he had her body X-rayed. It was Evita. In fact, Dr Ara's work was so good that even Evita's internal organs were preserved!

President Aramburu knew that if he destroyed the body, many people would be angry. Then Colonel Koenig, head of Army Intelligence, offered help. Shortly afterwards, in November 1955, the body disappeared.

Many stories started to go round Argentina about what had happened to Evita's body. Some said it was burned, others that it had been secretly buried.

When the next elections were held in February 1958, a new president came into power. Aramburu left the scene, and nothing more was heard of Evita's body for 12 years. Then, in 1970, Aramburu was murdered. After his death his lawyer handed over an envelope that contained the answer.

The musical
Evita's life is remembered in many books and in musical stage and film productions.

In September 1971, workers in an Italian cemetery were told to open the tomb of a woman called Maria Maggi de Magistris.

Inside was a perfectly preserved body. But the body was not Maria Maggi's. It was Evita Perón's. It had been secretly buried there 14 years earlier. Colonel Koenig had arranged it.

Juan Perón returned to Argentina in 1973 after his party won the elections. In September he was elected president again. However, he was in his late seventies by then, and the strain was too much for him. He died in July the following year. Evita's body was returned to Argentina, and the two coffins were shown side by side. In different ways, both she and her husband had come home after many years in exile. Evita's travels finally ended 24 years after her death when, in 1976, she was placed in her family tomb.

A musical about her life, written by Andrew Lloyd Webber, first opened in the 1970s. In 1996, this was turned into a film, with Madonna playing the part of the poor girl who rose to the very top. Today Evita is more famous than ever.

Resting place
Evita's body now rests in Recoleta Cemetery in Buenos Aires. It is said to be in a bombproof case.

Together again
In 1974, when Juan Perón died, he was not embalmed. His closed coffin was shown next to Evita's open one.

Evita's good works have never been forgotten.

Mummy paint
Mummies were
once used to make
a brown artists'
colour called
Caput Mortuum,
which means "dead
head" in Latin.

Mummies Today

In 1798 the French general Napoleon Bonaparte
invaded Egypt. This started a fashion for all
things Egyptian, first in France then in other
European countries. This was seen in clothes,
in furniture, in painting, music, and many other
areas of life. Teams of French scholars began to
study the ancient Egyptian civilization, and publi
interest grew even stronger when mummies were
packed up and sent back to France.

However, by this time, a lot of the evidence
had been destroyed. Over the centuries,
thousands of mummies had been burned as fuel,
ground up for medicine, or simply left to decay.

The first mummies sent to Europe were
treated little better. Many
were "unwrapped" at public
events. Although some
people attended out of
scientific interest, most
came to be horrified by what
might be inside when the
demonstrator had unrolled a
the bandages. Of course, this
type of performance
destroyed much of the
historical evidence that
the mummy could give.

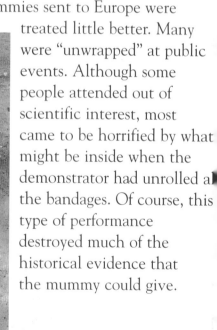

*Today, most scientists treat
the ancient dead respectfully
and make the information
they find widely available.*

44

Today, scientists use mummies to find out what diseases people suffered from in the past. They use microscopes to look at skin, bone, and other body tissues. It is also quite easy to scan the face of a mummy into a computer. You can then make some changes to allow for the passing of time, and produce an image of what the mummy looked like when alive. You can see the living face of an ancient Egyptian – at least on the screen.

Other advances in technology mean that people can take better care of ancient things that are found. In 1895, X-rays were discovered. An X-ray picture shows scientists what is inside a mummy coffin. Mummies can now be studied without being unwrapped.

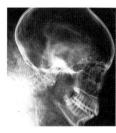

Aches and pains
This X-ray of an Inca mummy shows that the brain has become much smaller, and now lies at the bottom of the skull.

A mummy about to enter a CAT scanner.

Nowadays, scientists use electronic scanners, called CAT scanners, to produce three-dimensional images of a mummy inside its bandages. The machine can be set to show the mummy at different levels below the surface.

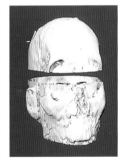

A look inside
This CAT scan shows the skin on a mummy's face. At another setting, the machine could show the bone beneath the skin.

Ever present
This is the clothed skeleton of Jeremy Bentham, a philosopher who died in 1832. His mummified head is between his feet.

While scientists are still studying ancient mummies, many people today still have their dead bodies preserved.

Sometimes, people want to see their dead relatives before they are buried. The bodies are embalmed so that they will last a short while. They are not intended to last forever.

But some are, and Evita Perón's mummy is not the only recent example. As in ancient Egyptian times, today's mummies are the bodies of rich or famous people.

In 1924, the Russian leader Vladimir Lenin died. His wife thought that his memory would best be kept alive by building houses, hospitals, and schools. However, Josef Stalin, the leader of the Soviet Union at the time, had other ideas. There was a tradition in Russia, as in many countries, of going to see the bones of dead saints. Since the Communist Party had replaced religion, Stalin felt it was only right that the people should have a substitute. So, Lenin's body was embalmed and placed inside a new building in Red Square, and people queued up to see the founder of the Soviet Union. The queues are rather shorter today, but people still go to see the body.

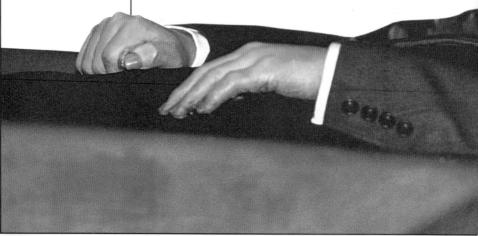

In the United States, people can pay to have their bodies frozen in liquid nitrogen. They hope that people living in the future will be able to bring them back to life.

This science is called cryogenics. Extreme cold is certainly the best way of preserving a body. We make use of this fact every time we put meat into a freezer, and some of the bodies in the best condition are those which have been found in cold countries. These range from Stone Age people to those more recently dead, such as the climber George Mallory, who was found on Mount Everest in 1999. He died trying to reach the top of the mountain in 1924.

The question of whether science could bring frozen bodies back to life has still to be answered. We know it can be done with bacteria. One day it may be possible with human beings, and some of us may live to see it.

Cryogenics
When people choose to be frozen after their deaths, their bodies are preserved in large steel containers.

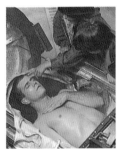

Sci-fi
Science fiction writers and movie-makers capture our imaginations with their ideas about how cryogenics might be used in the future.

The mummy of Vladimir Lenin

Glossary

abbey
A church with buildings beside it where religious men or women live.

afterlife
Some kind of life after death. Different civilizations have different beliefs about this.

ancient Egyptians
The people living in Egypt when it was ruled by pharaohs. This was between around 3000 BC and 300 BC.

bacteria
Very small living things. Some cause disease or break down dead bodies.

bog
A piece of land that is always wet and muddy.

CAT scanner
A computerized machine that produces three-dimensional images of a person's bones and organs.

cryogenics
The process of keeping bodies at very low temperatures so they cannot decay.

curse
A wish, usually spoken or written, intended to harm another person.

embalm
To use chemicals or perfumes to stop a body from decaying.

hieroglyphs
Pictures that stand for words or sounds. These were used in ancient Egyptian writing.

Inca
A South American civilization that lasted from 1200 to 1532, when it was destroyed by the Spanish.

intestines
Tubes in the body that carry food after it leaves the stomach.

litter
A bed, or stretcher, that can be carried. It is used to move people or mummies.

llama
A South American animal related to the camel. It is used for meat, wool, and transport.

monk
A man living and working in a religious group.

mummify
The process of making a body into a mummy.

mummy
A body that has been preserved by nature or by people.

natron
A natural salt used by the ancient Egyptians to dry bodies.

pharaoh
The name given to the kings of ancient Egypt, from 3000 BC to 300 BC

shrine
A thing that people build to help them remember a dead person. The body may be inside.

tomb
A large grave that is above the ground. It is usually decorated.

Tutankhamun
A boy pharaoh who ruled Egypt from about 1336 BC to 1327 BC. He was probably around 16 years old when he died.

underworld
The ancient Egyptians believed that everyone had to travel through this world beneath the earth on their journey to the afterlife.

X-rays
These can pass through only the soft parts of the body. They are used to make a picture of a person's bones and internal organs.